MW01166768

Shapes

Discovering Flats and Solids

by Michele Koomen

Consultant:
Deborah S. Ermoian
Mathematics Faculty
Phoenix College
Phoenix, Arizona

Bridgestone Books
an imprint of Capstone Press
Mankato, Minnesota

Bridgestone Books are published by Capstone Press
151 Good Counsel Drive, P.O. Box 669, Mankato, Minnesota 56002
http://www.capstone-press.com

Copyright © 2001 Capstone Press. All rights reserved.
No part of this book may be reproduced without written permission from the publisher.
The publisher takes no responsibility for the use of any of the materials
or methods described in this book, nor for the products thereof.
Printed in the United States of America.

Library of Congress Cataloging-in-Publication Data
Koomen, Michele.
　　Shapes: discovering flats and solids/by Michele Koomen.
　　p. cm.—(Exploring math)
　　Includes bibliographical references and index.
　　ISBN 0-7368-0820-5
　　1. Geometry—Juvenile literature. [1. Shape.] I. Title. II. Series.
QA445.5 .K66 2001
516—dc21   00-010563

Summary: Simple text, photographs, and illustrations introduce two- and three-
　　dimensional shapes including circles, squares, quadrilaterals, cylinders, and spheres,
　　and give examples of shapes in the real world.

Editorial Credits
Tom Adamson, editor; Lois Wallentine, product planning editor; Linda Clavel, designer;
　　Katy Kudela, photo researcher

Photo Credits
Capstone Press/Linda Clavel, cover, 9; CG Book Printers, 19
Gregg Andersen, 4, 10, 15, 16, 18, 21
Image Farm Inc., 12, 14
Photri-Microstock, 20 (top)
Unicorn Stock Photos/Kimberly Burnham, 7, 13 (bottom)
Visuals Unlimited/A. Gurmankin, 13 (top); Bill Beatty, 20 (bottom)

1 2 3 4 5 6 06 05 04 03 02 01

Table of Contents

Flats and Solids 5

Triangles 6

Quadrilaterals 8

Rectangles and Squares 10

Many Sides 12

Circles and Ovals 14

Spheres 17

Rectangular Solids 18

Shapes Are All around Us 20

Hands On: Make a Cube 22

Words to Know 23

Read More 24

Internet Sites 24

Index 24

2-D shapes (flats)

hexagon

quadrilateral

square

triangle

rectangle

octagon

pentagon

oval

circle

3-D shapes (solids)

cube

rectangular solid

sphere

cylinder

Flats and Solids

We see many shapes every day. Some shapes are two-dimensional (2-D). These shapes are flat. Other shapes are three-dimensional (3-D). They are solid. A solid has length, width, and height.

Triangles

A triangle is a flat shape with 3 straight sides and 3 corners. These shapes are triangles.

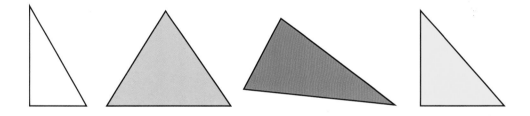

These shapes are not triangles. Why?

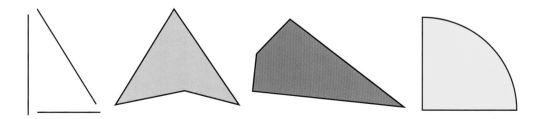

The sail on this sailboat is a triangle.

Quadrilaterals

A flat shape with 4 straight sides and 4 corners is a quadrilateral. These shapes are quadrilaterals.

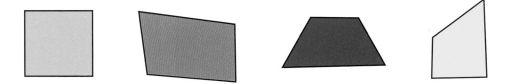

Which of these shapes are quadrilaterals?

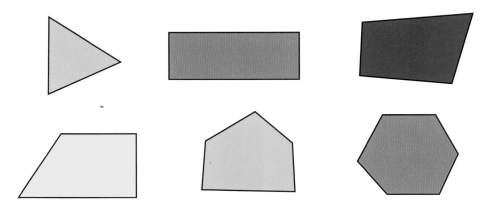

This kite is a quadrilateral.

Rectangles and Squares

Rectangles and squares are special quadrilaterals. The sides of a rectangle opposite each other are the same length. All the corners of a rectangle are the same. These envelopes are rectangles.

These crackers are shaped like squares. The four sides are all the same length. All the corners of a square are the same.

Many Sides

Some flat shapes have many sides. Stop signs have 8 sides. A flat shape with 8 sides is an octagon.

◀ Home plate has 5 sides. A flat shape with 5 sides is a pentagon.

Each shape in this honeycomb has 6 sides. A flat shape with 6 sides is a hexagon. ▶

13

Circles and Ovals

Circles and ovals are flat shapes that do not have corners. Circles are round. This sign is a circle.

This sign is an oval. An oval looks
like a stretched-out circle.

Spheres

A sphere is another kind of shape. It is not a flat shape. It is a round, solid shape. A globe is a sphere. Oranges, bubbles, and marbles also are spheres.

Rectangular Solids

A rectangular solid has six sides. Each side is called a face. Faces are flat shapes that make a solid shape. This box is a rectangular solid.

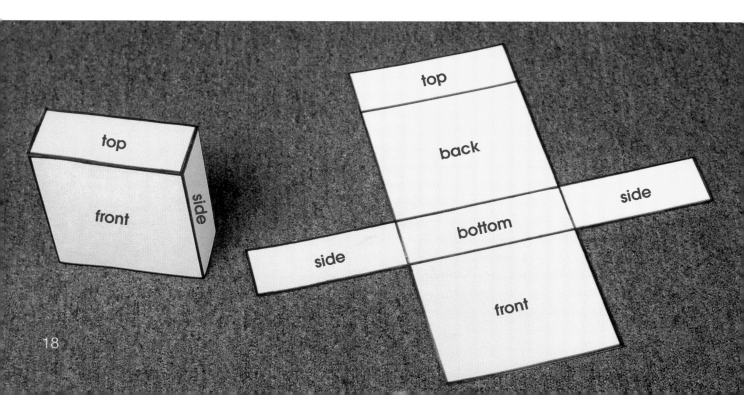

A cube is a special kind of
rectangular solid. All of a cube's
faces are squares. Dice are cubes.

These train cars are rectangular solids.

The roller on the front of this machine is a tube-shaped solid. It is called a cylinder.

This hopscotch game is made up of squares. What other shapes can you see in your neighborhood?

Hands On: Make a Cube

All of a cube's faces are squares.
You can make a cube out of paper.

What You Need

Pencil   Ruler
Paper   Scissors
Tape

What You Do

1. Draw a 2-inch (5-centimeter) square near the top of the paper.
2. Draw three more squares the same size below the first square.
3. Draw one square on each side of the second square. The squares should make a "t" shape like the drawing on this page.
4. Cut out the "t" shape.
5. Number the squares as shown in the drawing.
6. Fold the squares toward the center along the dotted lines, making good creases.
7. The square marked 1 is the bottom of your cube. The squares marked 2, 3, 4, and 5 are the four sides. The square marked 6 is the top.
8. Tape the sides together to form a box shape. Tape the top to each of the four sides.

Words to Know

cylinder (SIL-uhn-dur)—a tube-shaped solid with circular ends; a soup can is a cylinder.

hexagon (HEK-suh-gahn)—a flat shape with six straight sides

length (LENGKTH)—the distance from one end of something to the other

octagon (OK-tuh-gahn)—a flat shape with eight straight sides

pentagon (PEN-tuh-gahn)—a flat shape with five straight sides

quadrilateral (kwahd-ruh-LAT-ur-uhl)—any flat shape with four straight sides and four corners; squares and rectangles are quadrilaterals.

sphere (SFEEHR)—a round, solid shape like a ball

Read More

Adler, David A. *Shape Up!* New York: Holiday House, 1998.

Bryant-Mole, Karen. *Shapes.* Mortimer's Math. Milwaukee: Gareth Stevens, 2000.

King, Andrew. *Exploring Shapes.* Math for Fun. Brookfield, Conn.: Copper Beech Books, 1998.

Patilla, Peter. *Shapes.* Math Links. Des Plaines, Ill.: Heinemann Library, 2000.

Internet Sites

Ask Dr. Math
http://mathforum.com/dr.math
Figure This! Math Challenges for Families
http://www.figurethis.org
MathSteps
http://www.eduplace.com/math/mathsteps/index.html

Index

circle, 14–15
cube, 19
cylinder, 20
face, 18, 19
flat shape, 6, 8, 12, 13, 14, 17, 18
hexagon, 13
octagon, 12
oval, 14–15

pentagon, 13
quadrilateral, 8–9, 10
rectangle, 10
rectangular solid, 18–19, 20
solid shape, 17, 18
sphere, 17
square, 10–11, 19, 21
triangle, 6–7